BIOGRAPHY FROM

ANCIENT CIVILIZATIONS

LEGENDS, FOLKLORE, AND STORIES OF ANCIENT WORLDS

The Life and Times of

LEIF ERIKSSON

Mitchell Lane
PUBLISHERS

BIOGRAPHY FROM
ANCIENT CIVILIZATIONS
LEGENDS, FOLKLORE, AND STORIES OF ANCIENT WORLDS

TITLES IN THE SERIES

The Life and Times of

BIOGRAPHY FROM
ANCIENT CIVILIZATIONS
LEGENDS, FOLKLORE, AND STORIES OF ANCIENT WORLDS

The Life and Times of

LEIF ERIKSSON

Earle Rice Jr.

Mitchell Lane PUBLISHERS

Printing   1   2   3   4   5   6   7   8   9

Library of Congress Cataloging-in-Publication Data
Rice, Earle.
 The life and times of Leif Eriksson / by Earle Rice, Jr.
    p. cm. — (Biography from ancient civilizations)
 Includes bibliographical references and index.
 ISBN 978-1-58415-702-1 (library bound)
 1. Leiv Eiriksson, d. ca. 1020—Juvenile literature. 2. Explorers—America—Biography—Juvenile literature. 3. Explorers—Scandinavia—Biography—Juvenile literature. 4. America—Discovery and exploration—Norse—Juvenile literature. 5. Vikings—Juvenile literature. I. Title.
 E105.L47R53 2008
 973.01'3—dc22
                                                                              2008020921

ABOUT THE AUTHOR: Earle Rice Jr. is a former senior design engineer and technical writer in the aerospace, electronic-defense, and nuclear industries. He has devoted full time to his writing since 1993 and is the author of more than fifty published books, including *A Brief Political and Geographic History of Latin America: Where Are Gran Colombia, La Plata, and Dutch Guiana?, Blitzkrieg! Hitler's Lightning War, The Life and Times of Erik the Red*, and *Canaletto* for Mitchell Lane Publishers. Earle is listed in *Who's Who in America* and is a member of the Society of Children's Book Writers and Illustrators, the League of World War I Aviation Historians, the Air Force Association, and the Disabled American Veterans.

PUBLISHER'S NOTE: This story is based on the author's extensive research, which he believes to be accurate. Documentation of such research is contained on page 46.

 The internet sites referenced herein were active as of the publication date. Due to the fleeting nature of some web sites, we cannot guarantee they will all be active when you are reading this book.

 To reflect current usage, we have chosen to use the secular era designations BCE ("before the common era") and CE ("of the common era") instead of the traditional designations BC ("before Christ") and AD (*anno Domini*, "in the year of the Lord").

PHOTO CREDITS: Cover, pp. 1, 3, 6, 17, 26, 34, 36—Barbara Marvis; pp. 10, 16—Sharon Beck; p. 12—Mariner's Museum; p. 14—Ted Spiegel/National Geographic/Getty Images; p. 20—North Wind Picture Archives; p. 23—Tom Lovell/National Geographic/Getty Images; p. 28—Hulton Archives/Getty Images; p. 32—Archive Photos/Getty Images; p. 40—WebExhibits.

BIOGRAPHY FROM

ANCIENT CIVILIZATIONS

LEGENDS, FOLKLORE, AND STORIES OF ANCIENT WORLDS

CONTENTS

*For Your Information

This statue of Ingolf Arnarson keeps eternal watch over Iceland's capital city of Reykjavik. Ingolf and his foster brother Hjorleif settled on the island in about 970 CE. Hjorleif was killed during their first winter there; thus Ingolf has received sole credit for founding Iceland.

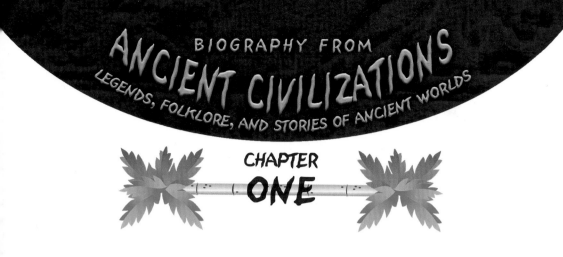
CHAPTER ONE

THE LONG WAIT

More than a millennium ago, probably sometime in the 940s CE, a son was born to Herjolf and his wife, Thorgerd, at their farm in Drepstokk, Iceland. They named their son Bjarni. He was a fourth-generation Icelander who could trace his ancestry back to his great-grandfather Herjolf, his father's namesake. The original Herjolf was a kinsman and friend of Ingolf Arnarson, Iceland's founder. In the mid-870s, Ingolf had allotted the land between Vog and Reykjanes to him. It was a good parcel of land, and it gave Herjolf the "settler" a solid start in a new and challenging land. Bjarni's great-grandfather prospered and passed along his wealth to his son, Bard Herjolfsson. Bard maintained his inheritance and in time passed it to his son, the second Herjolf, who could do no less.

From first breath, Herjolf's son Bjarni did not want for life's necessities. But he was not content to sit back in comfort and leisurely await a rich inheritance. Harnessing the power of ambition and hard work, Bjarni quickly developed into a self-made trader with unlimited potential. "He soon earned himself both a good deal of wealth and a good name," according to the *Saga of the Greenlanders*, "and spent his winters alternately abroad and with his father."[1] (*The Saga of the Greenlanders* and *Erik the Red's Saga* make up the *Vinland Sagas*, which tell the story of the Norse discovery and exploration of North America.)

At a young age, Bjarni established himself as a merchant of considerable means, voyaging back and forth across the treacherous waters between Iceland and Norway. "During the last winter Bjarni spent in Norway," the *Saga* goes on, "Herjolf [Bjarni's father] decided to accompany Eirik [Erik] the Red to Greenland and left his farm."[2] Erik the Red, a Viking explorer and settler, had led a party of between 400 and 500 Icelanders to form the first European settlements in Greenland in 986.

When Bjarni returned to Eyrar, Iceland, in the summer of that same year, he learned of his father's departure for the first time. Stunned by the news of his father's decision to emigrate to a land he knew almost nothing about, Bjarni refused to unload his cargo. His crew asked him why. He told them that he intended to continue his custom of spending alternate winters with his father. "I will take the ship to Greenland," he said, "if you will bear me company."[3] They agreed to abide by his decision.

Bjarni then cautioned them: "Our voyage must be regarded as foolhardy, seeing that no one of us has ever been in the Greenland Sea."[4] His warning did not alter their decision. They fitted out their ship—probably a *knörr*—for the voyage and put out to sea. A *knörr* is generally described as a Viking merchant ship, modeled along the lines of a traditional longship (warship). It differed from the oar-propelled longship in that it depended largely—if not entirely—on a single square sail set on a yard for propulsion. Bjarni and his crew sailed for three days before the land disappeared below the horizon.

Then, suddenly, the accompanying wind fell off. A dense fog fell upon them like a cold wet shroud. A fierce wind from the north seized their tiny ship and tossed it from wave to mountainous wave. Yet on they sailed, navigating without seeing, never knowing where they were or where they were going. They drifted aimlessly for many days.

Finally, the fog lifted and they could see the sun again. With the sun in view, they could now reestablish the quarters of the heavens: north, south, east, and west. By guess and instinct, they reshaped their course, hoisted their square sail, and sailed on for the rest of the day. At day's end, they sighted land—but just what land it was they knew not.

Bjarni and his crew speculated among themselves as to the land's identity. As for Bjarni, he strongly suspected it was not Greenland. His crew looked to him for direction. "It is my counsel," he said, "to sail close to the land."[5] They took his advice and sailed in toward the shore. Closer in, they could see a land of low hills and thick forests. This land did not match descriptions of Greenland that Bjarni had heard earlier. Deciding against landing, he told his crew to keep sailing. Keeping the shoreline to their port (left) side, they turned their sail landward and put out to sea again. Bjarni ordered them to sail north.

Catching a southerly wind, they left the unknown land behind. They sailed for two more days, then another land appeared on the port horizon. Was this Greenland at last? Bjarni's crew asked. He replied that he did not think so, because "there are said to be many large glaciers in Greenland."[6] Sailing in closer, they could see that the land was flat and wooded. The crew asked to go ashore to take on wood and water. Bjarni said no. "Ye have no lack of either of these,"[7] he said. He did not wish to risk the safety of his men in what might be a hostile land. His decision occasioned a round of complaints from his sea-weary men. When their grumblings subsided, they hoisted sail and headed north again.

Three days later, a third land came into view. It was high and mountainous and covered with glaciers. This land also did not match Bjarni's conception of Greenland. His crew again asked if he would land there. He said he would not, "because this land does not appear to me to offer any attractions."[8] Again his hardy Viking crew grumbled, but in fairness to Bjarni, he probably acted with their well-being at heart. They continued north along the coastline without lowering their sail and soon learned that the third land was an island. Leaving it astern, they returned to the open sea and sailed for another four days on the same accompanying wind.

On the fourth day, Bjarni and his wet and weary companions sighted yet a fourth large landmass dead ahead of them. Could this at long last be Greenland? the crew asked their master. Bjarni replied, "This land is most like what I have been told of Greenland, and we'll

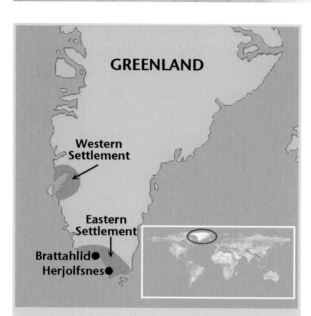

GREENLAND

Western Settlement

Eastern Settlement

Brattahlid●
Herjolfsnes●

In 986, Erik the Red founded Greenland with about 500 Viking settlers. Their two main settlements are shown here. Erik lived at Brattahlid; Bjarni Herjolf lived at Herjolfnes.

head for shore here."[9] As the sun slipped below the horizon, the weary voyagers landed along a headland where they had sighted a boat. By some odd stroke of luck, after sailing for hundreds of miles, Bjarni and the others had finally made land at precisely the location of his father's home. Herjolf had made his home on a small cape that was named for him. It was then (and still is) called Herjolfsnes (Herjolf's point).

Bjarni Herjolfsson did not know it then, but he and his Viking crew had sailed along the coast of a great continent. The world would someday come to know it as North America. Beyond question, it was the greatest voyage of his life. It was also his last. Bjarni had become the first positively identified European to sight North America. Thereafter, he quit his merchant voyages and joined his father at Herjolfsnes. They worked the farm together until Herjolf died. Bjarni then took over the farm and lived out his life there.

A little farther up the southwest coast of Greenland from Herjolfsnes, at a farmstead called Brattahlid, dwelled Erik the Red, founder of the island's first European settlements. Erik had established a reputation early on as something of a rollicking misfit, but he had since settled down to raise a family. At the time of Bjarni's circuitous voyage, Erik's second son was about six years old. The first European exploration and settlement of North America would have to wait for him to come of age. His name was Leif Eriksson.

Vikings in the North Atlantic

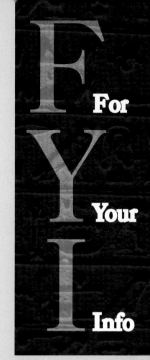

Vikings were perhaps best known as savage sea raiders from the north (Norway, Sweden, and Denmark). These Northmen (or Norsemen) terrorized the British Isles and much of Europe, from France to Russia and as far south as the Mediterranean Sea. They built their reputation for uncommon barbarity during three centuries known as the Viking Age (c.800 CE to c.1100 CE). Despite their popular image as seafaring warriors, most Vikings went raiding only occasionally. The majority of Vikings were primarily farmers and traders.

Early in the ninth century, probably because of an increasing population at home, these same farmers and traders began a westward expansion into the North Atlantic. Norwegians seeking more fertile lands to till or richer trade routes to exploit colonized Iceland in c.870. Erik the Red founded two settlements on Greenland in 986. That same year, Bjarni Herjolfsson discovered the coastline of North America by chance. His discovery opened the door for the first recorded European to land on the North American continent—several centuries before the Age of Discovery.

Considering the size and frailty of their ships, and their limited knowledge of navigational methods, Viking accomplishments in the North Atlantic fell just short of the impossible. The average *knörr,* an all-purpose merchant vessel, measured only 53.5 feet (16.3 meters) long, 18.7 feet (5.7 meters) wide, and 6.9 feet (2.1 meters) deep. It had a cargo capacity of up to 24 tons. Some were equipped with oars but most relied solely on the power of sails. Whenever possible, Vikings sailed close to land, where navigation posed no problems. When traversing open stretches of ocean—such as the waters from Norway to Iceland and beyond—they used very primitive methods to find their way. Sun and stars provided some guidance, as did basic bearing

The knörr, represented in this model, was the all-purpose merchant vessel of the Vikings.

dials and azimuth circles. The presence of birds and even whales sometimes served as oceangoing signposts. Mostly, they simply sailed to the latitude of their destination and followed the parallel until they sighted land.

Several centuries before the golden age of exploration, Vikings in the North Atlantic served notice to Europeans that a great new continent stood between them and the far side of the world.

This lifelike statue of Leif Eriksson guards a portal in the renowned Mariner's Museum in Newport News, Virginia. A determined figure—with jutting jaw and ax in hand—serves well his image as a true pathfinder.

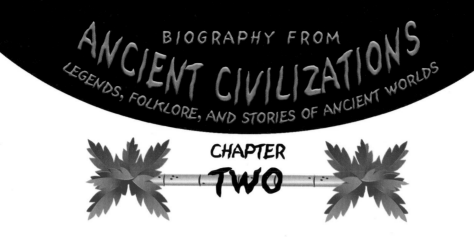
COMING OF AGE

Leif Eriksson (sometimes spelled Eiriksson or Ericson) is one of the most famous Vikings of all time. Even so, the details of much of his life remain sketchy at best. He was born near what is now Budardalur, Iceland, about 980 CE. His father was Erik the Red, who was himself renowned for establishing the first settlements in Greenland in 986. Erik's marriage to Thjodhild Jorundardottir yielded Leif and two other sons, Thorvald and Thorstein. At some point, Erik strayed, and his illicit affair with an unnamed mistress produced a daughter named Freydis Eiriksdottir. The order of birth for the four children is uncertain.

About 960, at the age of ten, Erik the Red left his native Norway for western Iceland with his father, Thorvald. Thorvald had been exiled "because of manslaughters,"[1] a polite way of saying he killed at least two men in a brawl. When Erik came of age, he became involved in a series of similar quarrels in which several men were killed. Like his father, now dead, Erik was convicted of "manslaughters" and banished from Iceland for a period of three years.

Erik decided to search the waters west of Iceland for a land that the Norwegian Gunnbjorn Ulfsson had skirted about eighty years earlier. He loaded both his family and livestock aboard ship and spent the next three years exploring the big island he came to call Greenland (in the hope that others would become attracted to it). When his period of exile expired, he sailed back to Iceland. Erik quickly recruited a large party of settlers to return to Greenland with him.

Twenty-five ships returned to Greenland with Erik. Several sank in the ice-filled waters along the way, and some turned back, but fourteen ships and about 450 colonists arrived safely. They established two colonies on the southwest coast of Greenland—the Eastern and Western Settlements. Erik selected for himself one of the nicest areas he had found earlier, at the head of Eiriksfjord in the Eastern Settlement, and built a farmstead there called Brattahlid. Erik presided over both settlements as the paramount chieftain of the island.

Leif Eriksson and his siblings presumably grew up at Brattahlid, but accounts of their early years went unrecorded. Leif's story essentially begins when he reached the age of maturity. In 999, at about age nineteen, he decided to visit the land of his ancestors. He

The ruins of Brattahlid, Erik the Red's home in the Eastern Settlement, overlook Eiriksfjord. Erik's son, Leif Eriksson, spent most of his boyhood here. After Erik's death, Leif lived out his life as the master of Brattahlid.

set sail for Norway that summer. En route, a high wind blew him astray and forced him to put in at the Hebrides, a group of islands west of Scotland. Then, oddly, the wind died off completely, keeping him becalmed in the Hebrides for the rest of the summer.

While waiting for the winds to return, Leif struck up an acquaintance with a local maiden of a good family named Thorgunna. Friendship ripened quickly into love. Toward the end of summer, the winds came up again, and Leif made ready to leave. As written in *Erik the Red's Saga*, Thorgunna asked to go with him. He asked if her family would agree to her leaving with him. She said she did not care. Leif told her that he thought it unwise to abduct a woman of such high birth in a foreign country, particularly since "there are so few of us"[2] (that is, himself and his crew).

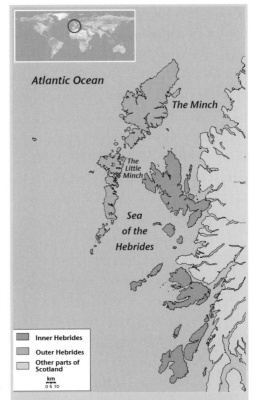

During the Viking Age, the Hebrides island group, off the west coast of Scotland, was the scene of frequent incursions by Norse settlers.

"I'm not sure you'll like the alternative better,"[3] Thorgunna replied.

"I'll take my chances on that,"[4] Leif said.

"Then I will tell you," she said, "that I am with child, and that this child is yours."[5] Now, Thorgunna was known for her ability to predict the future. She went on to tell him that her unborn child was a boy. Even though Leif chose to leave them, she said that she and her son would one day follow him and find him. She promised coldly that he would not like the experience. Leif left anyway—possibly with a coldness in his soul. Perhaps to warm Thorgunna's heart, he left her with a Greenland cape, an ivory belt, and a gold ring.

Sources vary as to whether Leif and Thorgunna ever met again. Some state that Leif later returned to the Hebrides for Thorgunna and their son, but Thorgunna's fate remains unclear. What is known for sure is that Leif's son, whose name was Thorgils, eventually made it to Greenland, where he was recognized and accepted by his father. Some say that Thorgils later showed signs of having his mother's ability to foresee the future. In any case, Leif left the Hebrides and reached Norway in the fall.

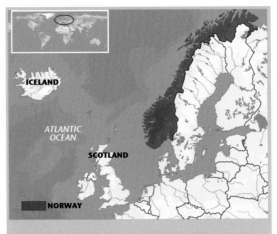

In 999, Leif Eriksson wintered in Norway as the guest of King Olaf I Tryggvason, who converted him to Christianity.

King Olaf I Tryggvason of Norway welcomed Leif to the homeland of his kinsmen. He liked Leif right away and invited him to spend the winter in his court. Leif had no wish to brave the North Atlantic in the cold season and accepted the king's cordial offer. Olaf had recently brought Christianity to Norway. A devout man, he proved a gracious host. The two men became good friends over the winter. Under the influence of the newly converted king, Leif renounced his pagan Norse gods—Odin, Thor, Vali, and many others—and converted to Christianity himself.

When spring drew near, Olaf asked his guest if he meant to sail back to Greenland soon. Leif said he did, whereupon the king asked him to carry the word of Christianity to the settlers in Greenland, including Leif's parents. Most Greenlanders were pagans. Leif told the king that most of them would resist the spread of Christianity. He doubted that he could successfully accomplish such a mission. Olaf replied that he could think of no man better suited to the task, adding, "[I]n thy hands the cause will surely prosper."[6]

"This can only be," Leif said, "if I enjoy the grace of your protection."[7] Olaf must have granted such assurance, for Leif returned to Greenland, bringing Christianity with him.

Leif sailed into Eiriksfjord and landed at Brattahlid. The name of his family home means "steep slope" for good reason: It stood on a sharp incline overlooking Eiriksfjord. Leif, who had been away for almost a year, climbed the slope to the turf-and-stone house of his father, Erik the Red. He found a warm welcome awaiting him. Leif began to spread the word about Christianity soon after his homecoming.

"He soon proclaimed Christianity throughout the land," wrote the unknown author of *Erik the Red's Saga*, "and the Catholic faith, and announced King Olaf Tryggvason's messages to the people, telling them how much excellence and how great glory accompanied his faith."[8]

Modern turf houses in Iceland are similar to those built by Erik the Red. Because of a scarcity of trees, Vikings built their homes of mainly turf and stone.

Leif's mother became one of his first converts to the religion of Christ. Thjodhild embraced Christianity with uncommon fervor, and ordered the construction of a building later known as Thjodhild's Church at some distance from the house. Thjodhild and neighboring converts met there regularly to offer prayers to their newly adopted deity.

Erik the Red did not share his wife's passion for Christianity. His refusal to join her in conversion so angered Thjodhild that she refused to share her bed with him until he did. Understandably, Erik the Red was "sorely vexed"[9] at this breach of marital privilege, but he continued to keep faith with the pagan gods of his Norse ancestry.

While Leif had been away, Greenlanders had begun to talk about the possibility of exploring the lands sighted by Bjarni Herjolfsson some fifteen years earlier. Leif listened with a keen ear about the forest-covered lands to the west and south. During his absence, he had come of age. Leif was now, according to the *Saga of the Greenlanders*, "a large, strong man, of very striking appearance and wise, as well as being a man of moderation in all things."[10] He no doubt recognized the rich potential open to those who could haul timber back to his barely green and nearly treeless homeland. Leif started at once to prepare for a western expedition.

Leif knew that the now-retired Bjarni no longer used his ship, so he journeyed to Herjolfsnes and bought it from him. He fitted his new ship with supplies and hired a crew of thirty-five. With everything ready, he asked his father to come along and head the expedition. Erik the Red declined at first but finally gave in to Leif's urgings. En route to the ship on the morning of their departure, Erik's horse threw him without warning. He injured his foot and could not continue. "I am not intended to find any other land than this one where we now live," Erik told Leif. "This will be the end of our travelling together."[11] He returned home to Brattahlid.

In the summer of 1001, Leif Eriksson sailed off into an epic adventure that would earn him a singular place in the world's history books.

Olaf I of Norway

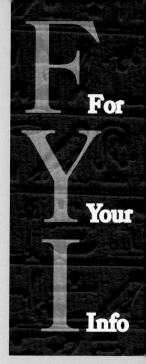

Except for members of Leif Eriksson's family, perhaps no one exerted a greater influence on his life than Olaf I, king of Norway from 995 to 1000. In 999, during what some might call Leif's "coming of age" voyage, he spent the winter in Olaf's court. During his short reign, Olaf I Tryggvason brought Christianity to Norway and converted young Leif to his faith. Leif sailed home in the spring of 1000. Acting as the king's messenger, Leif spread the word of Christianity throughout the settlements in Greenland.

Olaf was the son of Norwegian chieftain Tryggvi Olafsson and the great-grandson of Norwegian king Harald Fairhair. He was born about 968, shortly after his father was killed by Norwegian monarch Harald Graycloak. Legend has it that he fled with his mother to Russia, where he underwent training as a Viking warrior. Olaf put his training to good use in 991 when he led a Viking fleet in an attack against England. Ethelred II of England sued for peace and bought off the Vikings with large sums of *Danegeld* (tribute).

In 994, Olaf joined forces with Danish king Svein Forkbeard and invaded England again. Ethelred again bought peace with a large sum of Danegeld. In return, Olaf agreed to become a Christian and vowed never to attack England again. When Olaf was confirmed as a Christian, Ethelred acted as his godfather. Olaf kept his promise and never invaded England again. Instead, he used his newly acquired money to launch an invasion of his native Norway in 995. After the murder of Haakon the

Olaf becomes the first Christian king of Norway

Great, the last pagan king of Norway, the people accepted Olaf as their king.

Beginning in 996, Olaf I forcefully imposed Christianity on the areas of Norway he controlled—chiefly the coast and the western islands. He also commissioned a number of missionaries, including Leif Eriksson, to spread Christianity to the Shetland, Faeroe, and Orkney Islands, and to Iceland and Greenland.

In 1000, Olaf died during a sea battle with the Danish king Svein I (Svein Forkbeard, his former ally) and others at Svold (location unknown). Olaf leaped overboard from his flagship, the *Long Serpent,* and sank without a trace.

The discovery of grapes by Leif Eriksson's expedition to the North American continent led him to name the new land Vinland (Vine Land, or Wine Land).

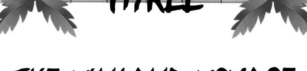

CHAPTER
THREE

THE VINLAND VOYAGE

Most of what the world knows about both Leif Eriksson and his father, Erik the Red, comes from Icelandic oral histories. Their stories were eventually written down by unknown authors in the *Saga of the Greenlanders* and *Erik the Red's Saga*. Together, these two tales make up the *Vinland Sagas*, which, as mentioned earlier, tell the story of the Norse discovery of North America.

Taken separately, these tales bear many similarities, but they also contain several significant differences. *The Saga of the Greenlanders* is generally considered the more accurate of the two. It was written about 1200 CE, two hundred years or more after the events it recalls, but some fifty to seventy-five years before *Erik the Red's Saga*. A key difference between them concerns the when and how of Leif Eriksson's landmark voyage.

In *Erik the Red's Saga*, the voyage occurs *by chance* when Leif is blown off course during his return voyage from Norway in 1000. Leif then retraces Bjarni Herjolfsson's route of some fifteen years earlier. By contrast, the *Saga of the Greenlanders* portrays the voyage as a *planned* expedition that left from Greenland in the summer of 1001—*after* Leif's return from Norway. This narrative follows the *Greenlanders* version.

In the summer of 1001, Leif and his crew of thirty-five hired hands set sail from Eiriksfjord. Leif set a course meant to retrace

Bjarni Herjolfsson's route *in reverse.* They "found first the land which Bjarni and his companions had last seen."[1] Sailing in close to shore, they cast anchor and put out a small boat. Leif and a few of his crew rowed ashore. They found a barren land with no grass. Large glaciers covered its highlands. From the glaciers all the way to the sea, the land looked like a single flat slab of rock. It seemed of little use for future settlements—but in landing there, Leif and his companions became the first Europeans to set foot in North America.

"As far as this land is concerned," Leif said, "it can't be said of us as of Bjarni, that we did not set foot on shore."[2] Leif named the desolate expanse Helluland (Flat Rock Land). The voyagers returned to their ship and put out to sea again. They soon sighted a second land. As before, they sailed in close, cast anchor, and made a second landing.

This land was flat and forested. It sloped gently toward the sea, where they found many beaches of white sand at water's edge. "This land," Leif declared, "will be named for what it has to offer and called Markland (Forest Land)."[3] Once again, they returned to their ship without delay and resumed their southward voyage.

According to the saga, Leif and his crew caught the northeast winds and sailed for two *doegr.* Here the confusion begins as to the location of their end destination. Scholars have been unable to interpret the meaning of the Norse word *doegr.* It is a unit of measurement of some sort, but whether it denotes time or distance remains unknown. In terms of an algebraic expression, they sailed either x miles/meters, or y hours/days/weeks, to reach z, their still-unresolved destination.

At the end of this time/distance, they landed on an island that lay north of a main body of land. The weather was fine, and dew glistened on the deep grass. They collected the moisture in their hands and marveled at its sweetness. After a brief look around, they returned to their ship and sailed into the sound separating the island and a cape that jutted out northward from the mainland. Rounding the cape, they sailed westward and soon ran aground in the shallows at low tide. To the stranded Vikings, the sea looked far, far away.

Eager to explore the new land that seemed to beckon them invitingly, Leif and his comrades could not wait for the incoming tide to refloat their *knörr*. They rowed ashore through the shallows in their small boat and began their exploration where a river flowed into the sea from a lake. When the incoming tide refloated their ship, they rowed back to it and sailed up the river and on into the lake. They hauled their sleeping sacks ashore and built booths (temporary shelters). Leif liked the location so much that he decided to spend the winter there, and they began to build large houses.

Here was a land that seemed quite possibly as close to paradise as these weathered Vikings would ever come. The river and lake abounded with salmon, larger than any of them had ever laid eyes on. Their livestock would need no fodder for the winter—the temperature never fell below freezing, and the grass withered only slightly. Unlike Greenland or Iceland, the days and nights stayed near-equal in length.

Vikings come ashore in Vinland, prepared for a lengthy stay. They often brought their entire families and all their belongings with them on exploratory or colonizing voyages.

In midwinter, they could see the sun at midmorning and in midafternoon.

When they finished building their permanent houses, Leif spoke to his men: "I propose now to divide our company into two groups, and to set about an exploration of the country."[4] For security reasons, Leif, a wise and prudent man, directed half his crew to guard their encampment while the other half investigated the land. He further ordered the explorers to stay close enough to return to camp that same night. He also emphasized that they should always remain together. Leif himself alternated duties with his men, at times exploring and at other times guarding the camp.

One evening Leif learned that one of his crew, a German named Tyrker, had not returned from an exploring party. Tyrker had been like a second father to Leif when he was growing up. Leif assembled a search party and set out to find him. Not far from their winter camp they met Tyrker, a short, frail man with a large forehead and darting eyes. He was not lost at all and had a startling discovery to announce. "I have found vines and grapes,"[5] he said. The others expressed disbelief, but Tyrker knew what he had found. "I was born where there is no lack of either grapes or vines,"[6] he said.

After a good night's sleep, Leif assigned a new task to his men. "We will now divide our labors, and each day will either gather grapes or cut vines and fell trees," he said, "so as to obtain a cargo of these for my ship."[7] By the first signs of spring, the ship rode low in the water under the weight of a load of timber. The small boat that was drawn behind the ship was heaped with grapes. While his crew made the ship ready to sail, Leif looked at the land one last time and named it for Tyrker's discovery. He called it Vinland (Vine Land, or Wine Land). In the spring of 1002, Leif and his shipmates sailed for home.

Many scholars now believe that the lands they left behind—Vinland, Markland, and Helluland—are present-day Newfoundland, Labrador, and Baffin Island, respectively. Of the three, Vinland stirs the most controversy. Some historians fix its location in Cape Cod, Massachusetts, while others place it as far south as Florida. Newfoundland became the choice of many after Norwegian

Baffin Island

Yukon
Whitehorse
Northwest
Territories
Nunavut
Iqaluit
Yellowknife
Newfoundland and Labrador
British
Columbia
Alberta
Saskatchewan
Manitoba
Quebec
St.
John's
Edmonton
Victoria
Charlottetown
Prince
Edward
Island
Fredericton
Regina
Winnipeg
Ontario
Québec
Halifax
Present-Day
Ottawa
New
Brunswick
Nova
Scotia
CANADA
0 250 500 750 1000km
Toronto

The Viking voyages of exploration included the eastern seaboard of Canada, in the areas of present-day Baffin Island, Labrador, Newfoundland, and points south.

archaeologists found the remains of a Norse settlement dating to Leif's time in L'Anse aux Meadows (lahns-oh-MEH-dohz) in the early 1960s. Still, because of differences between old descriptions of the location and current conditions, uncertainty continues to obscure Vinland's true identity.

The Viking colonists caught a fair wind that lasted until they came within sight of Greenland and its glacier-covered mountains. About then, Leif saw something else in the rolling seas ahead that the others did not. As they sailed on close to the wind, they could first make out a skerry (reef)—and then fifteen people who were clearly stranded on it. Leif shouted to them and asked who was in charge. A man named Thorir, a Norwegian, claimed to be their leader. "And what is your name?"[8] he asked. Leif identified himself.

L'Anse aux Meadows, a small Viking Age settlement at the northern tip of Newfoundland, provides the only certain archaeological evidence that the Vikings reached the Americas before Columbus. Its discovery in the 1960s confirmed accounts of Norse voyages in the Viking sagas.

"Are thou a son of Erik the Red of Brattahlid?"[9] he inquired. Leif said he was.

"Now I want to invite all of you," Leif said, "to come on board my ship, bringing as much of your valuables as the ship can carry."[10] Thorir and his party, including his wife, Gudrid, clambered aboard with their gear. Leif delivered them all to a safe landing at Brattahlid. For his part in the "daring" rescue of the fifteen, he was ever after called Leif the Lucky. Some might feel that Thorir and his group were the lucky ones.

At Brattahlid, Leif invited Thorir, Gudrid, and three others to spend the winter with him. He also found lodging for all the other crew members. The long Vinland voyage was at last over, and Leif and his companions looked forward to a warm winter at home. Instead, in the Greenland settlements, the winter of 1002–1003 turned hot with fever.

Voyage to Nowhere

In *Erik the Red's Saga,* the unknown author describes a starkly different version of Leif's Vinland discoveries. He portrays them as occurring by chance after Leif was blown off course during his homeward voyage from Norway in the spring of 1000. This version allots only two short paragraphs to cover Leif's Vinland voyage, as well as his recovery of the fifteen Norwegians stranded on a reef. Upon Leif's return to Brattahlid, *Erik the Red's Saga* goes on to state: "After this there was much talk about making ready to go to the land which Leif had discovered."[11] This account names Thorstein, another son of Erik the Red, as a key advocate of a second exploratory voyage to Vinland.

Thorstein was "a worthy man, wise and much liked."[12] He and others valued Erik the Red's luck and foresight. They urged him to

Leif Eriksson meets with Native Americans in Vinland. His father, Erik, never made it to this western land.

accompany them on the voyage. Erik put them off for a time, but he eventually agreed to go with them. On the day of their sailing, Erik fell from his horse on the way to the ship, much as he does in the *Greenlanders* tale. According to this account, however, he "broke his ribs and injured his shoulder,"[13] rather than injuring his foot. Despite his injuries, Erik joins Thorstein and the others in what this version calls the second Vinland voyage.

In a ship belonging to Thorbjorn, a friend of Erik's, they sailed out of Eiriksfjord in high spirits, confident of a successful voyage. But when they arrived in the open sea, rough waters tossed them about in their tiny ship for a long time. They strayed far from their desired bearing. Instead of Vinland, they at last sighted Iceland and also saw a few birds from Ireland. Realizing how far they had strayed, they gave up on their voyage and headed for home. They arrived back in Greenland in the fall, worn out from battling an ill-tempered sea. From the outset, the second voyage to Vinland turned out to be a voyage to nowhere.

Amid high seas and decks awash, Leif Eriksson points to a new land in this artist's dramatic rendition of Leif's discovery of North America. A crew member looks on, perhaps too excited to worry about being swept overboard.

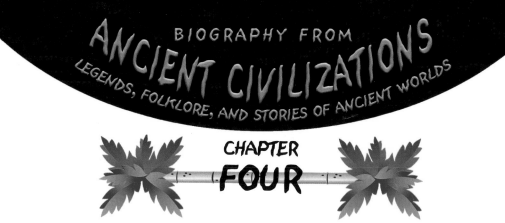
CHAPTER
FOUR

A TALE OF TWO BROTHERS

Summer, fall, winter, spring—all seasons seemed to merge seamlessly together in the Icelandic sagas. Seasons often changed in a word or in the turn of a quaintly affected phrase. In the *Saga of the Greenlanders,* the winter following Leif's return from Vinland took only two sentences to cover: Thorir and his crew died from an unnamed illness; and Erik the Red also died, presumably from the same malady. Historians speculate that their deaths came as a result of an epidemic introduced by a ship from Norway about that time. Diseases causing widespread fever and death were quite common in medieval Europe. In any case, the saga moves on quickly to tell of a great discussion of Leif's Vinland voyage.

Leif's brother Thorvald felt that Vinland warranted a lot more exploration. Leif must have agreed, for he offered the use of his ship to his brother and told him to have at it. Leif surely must have planned to return to Vinland himself, because he chose to lend his houses there to later explorers and settlers rather than to sell them. But the death of his father left him to administer not only Brattahlid but the settlements as a whole. Leif never saw Vinland again. Thorvald, on the other hand, felt more than willing to visit Vinland in his brother's place. He assembled a crew of thirty shipmates, made the ship ready, and put to sea in the spring of 1002 CE (or possibly a year later).

Thorvald. After Leif Eriksson's famous voyage of discovery in 1000 CE, his brother Thorvald landed in Vinland two—or possibly three—years later.

Details of their expedition went unrecorded until they reached Vinland. They found Leif's camp, apparently without difficulty, where they laid up their ship and settled in for the winter. Coastal waters and numerous rivers and lakes swelled with fish and kept them well fed during the cold months. In the spring of 1003, Thorvald and part of his crew explored to the west of their encampment in their small boat. They found fine forested lands with narrow white beaches. In their wanderings, they passed many islands in broad stretches of shallow waters. Nowhere did they find signs of animals, and only on one westerly island did they find evidence of humans—a hand-hewn wooden grain cover. That fall, they returned to Leif's houses to spend a second winter.

Winter passed without event. Thorvald and his companions spent the second summer exploring the country to the east in Leif's ship. Ill fortune struck when a sudden storm drove them ashore and smashed the keel of their ship on a ness (headland or point). There they stayed for a long time, repairing the damage. Before they left, Thorvald told his companions, "I want us to raise the broken keel up on this point and call it Kjalarnes (Keel point)."[1] And they did.

They continued their explorations to the east, and in one of the fjords (inlets) they came upon a forest-covered point that extended seaward. It caught Thorvald's eye at once. He led his crewmates ashore for a closer look. "Here it is beautiful," he told them, "and here would I like to raise my dwelling."[2] On their return to the ship, they discovered nine Native Americans hiding under upturned, hide-covered boats. The Vikings called the Native Americans *skraelings* (meaning "surly, ill-bred persons"). Assuming they were hostile, Thorvald and his men caught all but one and promptly killed them. One skraeling escaped in his canoe and apparently went to warn his people of the Norse intruders.

After the day's excitement, the Vikings camped on the point and fell exhausted into a deep sleep, unaware of the dangers developing nearby. Here, their story takes on a supernatural twist, as Icelandic tales often do. They were later awakened from their deep slumber by a mysterious cry from above their makeshift camp. An otherworldly voice shouted an urgent warning to Thorvald and his crew: "Awake, Thorvald, thou and all thy company, if thou wouldst save thy life; and board thy ship with all thy men, and sail with all speed from the land!"[3]

They fled to their ship at once. A swarm of skin canoes was already bearing down on them from across the inlet. Once aboard, Thorvald began issuing orders to the men: "We must put out the war-boards on both sides of the ship, and defend ourselves to the best of our ability, but offer little attack."[4] The men quickly lined both sides of the ship with shields, even as arrows from the attacking skraelings flew thick and fast. A spirited fight ensued, but the attackers quickly expended their arrows and fled.

Thorvald took stock of his men and found that none had been wounded. Thorvald was not so fortunate. "I have been wounded in my armpit," he told them. "An arrow flew in between the gunwale and the shield, below my arm. [A gunwale, pronounced GUH-nul, is the upper edge of a ship's side.] Here is the shaft, and it will bring me to my end."[5] Thorvald advised his men to prepare for their return voyage quickly, then asked them to bury him on the promontory he had selected as his future homesite. "You will bury me there and mark my grave with crosses at the head and foot, and call the spot Krossanes (Cross point) after that."[6] And then Thorvald died—possibly as one of Leif's converts to Christianity.

*Thorvald's expedition to Vinland ended in tragedy. During a spirited fight with **skraelings** (Native American attackers), Thorvald was struck by a hostile arrow in his armpit and died.*

Thorvald's men carried out his dying wishes, then rejoined the rest of the party at their original camp. The two groups exchanged news and spent the winter loading Leif's ship with grapes and grapevines. In the spring of 1004, they returned to Eiriksfjord. They had lots of news to tell Leif—and Leif had some news for them.

While Thorvald's companions had been away, Leif's other brother Thorstein had married Gudrid Thorbjarnardottir, the attractive blond daughter of Erik the Red's friend Thorbjorn. She was also the widow of Thorir, the Norwegian whom Leif had rescued from the skerry. When Thorstein Eriksson heard of Thorvald's demise, he wanted to go at once to Vinland to retrieve his brother's body. He raised a crew of twenty-five strapping men and set sail for Vinland. Gudrid went with them. The land had barely slipped below the horizon when the heaving waters seized their ship and tossed them about all summer.

Winter had entered its second week when the hapless Vikings finally reached land again, in Lysufjord in the Western Settlement. Thorstein somehow found lodging for all his crew; he and Gudrid stayed on their ship. One day, another man named Thorstein—a local farmer called Thorstein the Black—came by and invited them to stay with him and his wife, Grimhild. They gratefully accepted his invitation.

Early in the winter of 1004, an illness struck several of Thorstein's shipmates and many of them died. Thorstein ordered their bodies secured aboard ship to be returned to Eiriksfjord for burial in the summer. The illness spread rapidly and soon came to the house of Thorstein the Black. Grimhild bowed first to the disease and soon died. The malady next gripped Thorstein Eriksson. His condition quickly worsened, and he also died. At this turn of events, the saga recounts another supernatural occurrence.

The now-dead body of Thorstein Eriksson rose up and said, "Where is Gudrid?"[7] Thorstein the Black answered for the shocked Gudrid and asked what his namesake wanted. Thorstein replied, "I wish much to tell Gudrid her fortune, in order that she may be the better reconciled to my death, for I have come to a good resting place."[8] He went on to foretell her fate, which included another marriage, more children, a long life, much travel after the death of her husband, and ultimately her death as a nun in Iceland. Oddly or otherwise, Thorstein's prophecy came to pass.

As strange as such happenings appear to today's readers, they are in keeping with the superstitious beliefs of the time. Sir Walter Scott, the eighteenth-century Scottish writer, commented about the appearance of such events: "Such incidents make an invariable part of the history of a rude age, and the chronicles which do not afford these marks of human credulity, may be grievously suspected as being deficient in authenticity."[9] However far-fetched these ghostly

Lysufjord in the Western Settlement. In the winter of 1004, a terrible illness struck Thorstein Eriksson and his shipmates during their stay in Lysufjord. The disease spread quickly and soon infected Thorstein, who succumbed to the illness.

occurrences may seem today, they appeared very real to Vikings of Leif Eriksson's time.

In the spring of 1005 (or possibly 1006), Thorstein the Black accompanied Gudrid and the bodies of the dead home to Brattahlid. The dead were buried near the church now known as Thjodhild's Church. Gudrid went to live with her brother-in-law, Leif.

So ended a tale of two brothers. Of Erik the Red's children, only Leif and his half sister, Freydis, remained. What happened next to Gudrid and Freydis completes the story of the Vinland voyages and forms a tale of good and evil.

The Vinland Debate

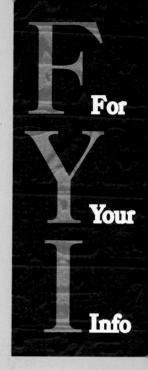

More than a thousand years after Leif Eriksson set foot in North America in 1000 CE, historians, scholars, and scientists continue to debate Vinland. Despite the aid of modern technology, they cannot agree on the meaning of its name or its location. Most scholars believe that *Vinland* means "Vine Land" or "Wine Land," named for the grapes and grapevines found there by Leif and his followers. Others argue that *vin* with a short *i* means "grassland" or "meadow" in Norwegian, hence *Vinland* might mean "Meadow Land." A misunderstanding of what the Vikings intended the name to mean has a direct bearing on the possible location of Vinland.

Scholars agree that evidence that might help locate Vinland with certainty is confusing and conflicting. Using the geographic landmarks described in the Icelandic sagas, a convincing case for Vinland's location can be made for both the northern tip of Newfoundland and the southern coast of Cape Cod, Massachusetts. Lyme grass grows along shores as far south as Cape Cod, and the length of days and nights is more equal there in the winter than farther north. Grapes no longer grow wild north of Cape Cod, but the earth was experiencing a warming cycle in Leif's time. Moreover, the wild grapes referred to in the sagas may actually have been red currants, gooseberries, or mountain cranberries.

Because of today's northern limits on the growth of wild grapes, many scholars favor Cape Cod as the most likely location of Vinland. With the discovery of the remains of a Norse settlement in L'Anse aux Meadows in the early 1960s, Newfoundland became the popular choice for Vinland's location. Considering that lyme grass grows there, and that *L'Anse aux Meadows* means "the cove at the

Leif Eriksson's voyage to Vinland retraced Bjarni Herjolfsson's earlier route in reverse.

meadows (or grasslands)," the argument for Newfoundland seems compelling. It also seems unlikely that the debate over Vinland's location will end anytime soon.

This statue of Gudrid and her son Snorri Thorfinnsson stands in stark isolation in the national park in Laugarbrekka, Snaefellsnes, Iceland. Snorri claimed distinction as the first European child born in North America.

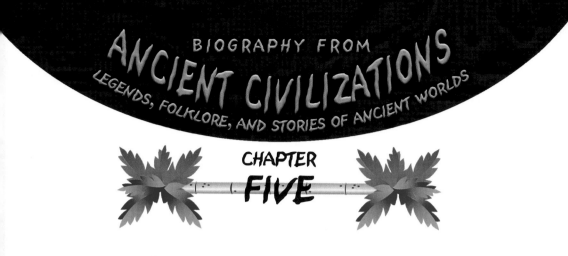
GUDRID AND FREYDIS

In the summer of 1005 CE, soon after Gudrid went to live in the house of Leif Eriksson at Brattahlid, a ship arrived from Norway. Its captain was the wealthy Thorfinn Karlsefni. Leif invited the eligible young bachelor to spend the winter with him at Brattahlid. Over the long winter months, Thorfinn became attracted to the lovely blond Gudrid and spoke to her of marriage. She told him to seek Leif's permission for her hand. Leif consented, and they were wed that same winter.

Come spring, all the talk in the settlement centered on another voyage to Vinland with intentions of establishing a colony there. Leif and a number of others, including Gudrid, urged Thorfinn to undertake such an expedition, and he did. He hired a crew of sixty men and five women. They loaded Thorfinn's ship with supplies and various kinds of livestock and made ready to sail. Thorfinn promised them all an equal share of anything of value that might come of their enterprise. He asked for Leif's houses in Vinland, but Leif again would only agree to lend them. At the appointed time, Thorfinn, Gudrid, and the crew set sail for the land of vines and grapes in the spring of 1006.

Fair winds and calm seas sped them on their way, and they arrived safely a short time later at the site of Leif's houses in Vinland. As an added stroke of good fortune, they found the carcass of a fine, large rorqual, a type of whale, stranded on the beach. Coupled with an abundance of natural bounty—all sorts of fish and game, and grapes, lots of grapes—the carved-up whale provided extra insurance against the scarcities of winter. Without ado of any sort, winter came and went. Signs of trouble first appeared in the summer of 1007.

A large group of men—skraelings—came out of the woods near the animal pasture, causing the Vikings' bull to bellow. Frightened, the skraelings ran toward Thorfinn's house to take cover, but he would not let them in. Then, in a show of good intentions, they took off their packs and offered goods in exchange for weapons. Thorfinn forbade his men to trade weapons. Instead, the skraelings settled for milk and milk products. The inability of the Vikings and the skraelings to understand each other's language did little to smooth the bartering process. With their stomachs filled with milk and cheese, the natives finally left. Thorfinn immediately ordered a palisade (fence of stakes) built around his farm.

At about this time, Gudrid presented Thorfinn with a baby boy. They named their son Snorri. Thorfinn now had even more to defend.

In late autumn of 1007, the skraelings returned in much greater numbers than before, but with the same trade goods. They again attempted to trade for weapons, and a scuffle broke out. One of the Vikings killed a native, and the rest of them fled. Thorfinn began at once to prepare for their return. "We have to decide on a plan," he told the others, "since I expect they will return for a third time, hostile and in greater numbers."[1]

Thorfinn outlined a plan to ambush the skraelings in a clearing with water on one side and a forest on the other. When the skraelings entered the clearing in force, the Vikings attacked, their snorting bull spearheading their charge as a four-legged tank of sorts. A savage fight ensued, and many skraelings died that day. The survivors fled and did not return again.

Thorfinn and his companions stayed in Vinland that winter, but in the spring of 1008 (or possibly later), he told the others that he wished to stay there no longer and wanted to return to Greenland. Those who wished to return with him loaded his ship with grapevines, berries, and skins, and they left for Eiriksfjord, where they spent the winter. Thorfinn made several more voyages before retiring to a mansion he had built in Iceland. There he and his family lived in high style until he died.

Gudrid, now a widow for the third time, went on a pilgrimage to Rome with her son, Snorri. After a visit with Pope Benedict VIII, she returned to Iceland and entered a convent, much as Thorstein had foretold. Snorri eventually became master of his father's estate and the perpetuator of a long line of noble descendants. Here ends Gudrid's tale.

About the time Thorfinn Karlsefni returned from Vinland in the summer of 1008, a ship arrived in Greenland from Norway. Two Icelandic brothers named Helgi and Finnbogi owned and captained the ship. Because of Thorfinn's considerable profit and fame, talk about another voyage to Vinland had been running high in the settlements.

Freydis proposed such a voyage to the brothers. They would use their ship and hers, with each to receive a half share of any profits from the venture. The two Icelanders agreed to this. Freydis then went to her half brother, Leif, and asked him for his houses in Vinland. Leif responded as before: He would lend—but not give—them to her.

Preparations for the voyage went ahead. The agreement between Freydis and the two brothers called for each ship to bring thirty fighting men and some women. Freydis cheated on their agreement from the start. Unknown to Helgi and Finnbogi, she smuggled aboard her ship five more men than the agreed-upon thirty. The thirty-five men included her husband, Thorvard. After agreeing to try to stick together, the brothers and Freydis set sail in separate ships. The brothers arrived before Freydis and moved their gear into Leif's house. When Freydis got there soon afterward, she scolded them for moving in: "It was to me that Leif loaned the house," she said, "and not to you."[2]

Helgi, no doubt surprised by her unexpected rudeness, said, "We brothers cannot hope to rival thee in wrong dealing."[3] He and Finnbogi gathered up their belongings and built a longhouse farther

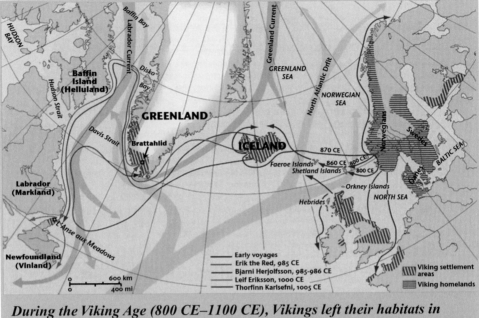

During the Viking Age (800 CE–1100 CE), Vikings left their habitats in Scandinavia, mostly to search for wealth and adventure not available to them at home. They first sailed south to England and northern Europe, then braved the North Atlantic to sail west. They ventured as far south as Vinland, which may have been Newfoundland.

from the sea by the side of a lake. In the meantime, Freydis had trees felled and timber loaded onto her ship. Soon, winter set in. For a time, the two camps held games for entertainment, but they quickly ended in disagreements and resentments. Each group kept to its own houses for most of the winter.

Early one morning, Freydis arose and went to the longhouse of the two brothers. In a seemingly agreeable manner, she approached Finnbogi about trading ships, for she wished to return to Greenland with a larger load of timber than her ship could carry. With hopes of mending their torn relationship, Finnbogi said, "To this I must accede, if it is thy pleasure."[4] On this cordial note, they parted.

Freydis returned to her house and awakened Thorvard with a wild tale about being struck and roughed up by the two brothers. "I am now paying the price for being so far from my home in Greenland," she wailed, "and unless you avenge this, I will divorce you."[5]

Thorvard, though a weak man, could no longer ignore her scolding. He assembled and armed his fighting men—five more than those of the other camp—and they all fell silently upon the longhouse of the brothers, who were asleep inside. Thorvard and his men bound up the brothers and the members of their camp before they could come fully awake, and led them outside. Freydis ordered each one of the men slain. Only the women remained, for no one would kill them.

Freydis did not falter. "Hand me an axe,"[6] she demanded. Someone did, and Freydis slew five women with a few swipes of the weapon.

After this wicked act, they all went back to their house. Freydis appeared quite pleased with her accomplishments, but she was already looking ahead. She warned everyone present never to tell of the morning's events upon their return to Greenland, on pain of death: "We will say that they remained behind here when we took our leave."[7]

When Freydis returned to her home and livestock in Greenland, she rewarded her group handsomely to keep them quiet. Even so, word of her savagery leaked out and followed her all the days of her life. Freydis Eiriksdottir died very much hated. Her story ends here, but her evil lives on in legend.

Of Erik the Red's children, now only Leif remained. He lived out his life as the master of Brattahlid, a wise and respected gentleman. He died about 1020, leaving his son Thorkell to carry the family tradition forward. Whether or not the mystery of the true location of Vinland is ever resolved, Leif Eriksson will always be remembered as the first European to set foot in North America—five hundred years before Christopher Columbus.

Atlantic Puffins

The Vinland Map

In 1957, a rare-book dealer in New Haven, Connecticut, bought an old and yellowed map from an Italian bookseller for $3,600. The bookseller claimed that it was a fifteenth-century *mappa mundi* (map of the world), supposedly redrawn from a thirteenth-century original. It showed Europe, Africa, and Asia. More important, however, it depicted a large island west of Greenland in the North Atlantic labeled "Vinlanda." A notation on the map described the island as the region that Vikings had visited in the eleventh century. If authentic, the map would further confirm that Christopher Columbus was not the first European to discover North America.

The authenticity of the Vinland Map became the subject of intense scrutiny. Map scholars from Yale University and the British Museum studied it for seven years. Finally, in 1965, they declared the map to be genuine. Yale University bought the map that same year, reputedly for one million dollars. Its authenticity remained unchallenged for only a year.

In 1966, an international commission convened at the Smithsonian Institution in Washington, D.C., for an in-depth review of the map's validity. The commission recommended that the map be subjected to scientific analysis. Yale hired Walter McCrone, a leading analytical chemist, to study the map. Using polarized light microscopy, he discovered anatase (titanium dioxide) in the ink, in a form allegedly not used in ink until the 1920s. In 1974, McCrone declared that the map might be a forgery.

Numerous scholarly and scientific studies followed over the next three decades with differing conclusions, both pro and con, as to the map's authenticity. In 2003, a study by Jacqueline S. Olin of the Smithsonian Institution, citing medieval ink-making methods, concluded that the map was genuine. Other scholars immediately refuted Olin's findings. Today—like the true location of Vinland—the authenticity of the Vinland Map remains unresolved.

CHAPTER NOTES

Chapter 1. The Long Wait

1. Örnólfur Thorsson, ed., *The Sagas of Icelanders: A Selection* (New York: Penguin Books, 2001), p. 636.

2. Ibid.

3. Arthur Middleton Reeves, North Ludlow Beamish, and Rasmus B. Anderson, *The Norse Discovery of America,* http://www.sacred-texts.com/neu/nda/nda08.htm

4. Ibid.

5. Ibid.

6. Thorsson, p. 637.

7. Reeves et al.

8. Ibid.

9. Thorsson, p. 638.

Chapter 2. Coming of Age

1. John Sephton, translator, *The Project Gutenberg eBook of Eirik the Red's Saga, by Anonymous,* http://www.gutenberg.org/files/17946/17946-h/17946-h.htm

2. Örnólfur Thorsson, ed., *The Sagas of Icelanders: A Selection* (New York: Penguin Books, 2001), p. 660.

3. Ibid.

4. Ibid.

5. Ibid.

6. Arthur Middleton Reeves, North Ludlow Beamish, and Rasmus B. Anderson, *The Norse Discovery of America,* http://www.sacred-texts.com/neu/nda/nda08.htm

7. Ibid.

8. Ibid.

9. Ibid.

10. Thorsson, p. 640.

11. Ibid., p. 638.

Chapter 3. The Vinland Voyage

1. Örnólfur Thorsson, ed., *The Sagas of Icelanders: A Selection* (New York: Penguin Books, 2001), p. 638.

2. Ibid.

3. Ibid., p. 639.

4. Arthur Middleton Reeves, North Ludlow Beamish, and Rasmus B. Anderson, *The Norse Discovery of America,* http://www.sacred-texts.com/neu/nda/nda08.htm

5. Ibid.

6. Ibid.

7. Ibid.

8. Thorsson, p. 641.

9. Reeves et al.

10. Thorsson, p. 641.

11. John Sephton, translator, *The Project Gutenberg eBook of Eirik the Red's Saga, by Anonymous,* http://www.gutenberg.org/files/17946/17946-h/17946-h.htm

12. Ibid.

13. Ibid.

Chapter 4. A Tale of Two Brothers

1. Örnólfur Thorsson, ed., *The Sagas of Icelanders: A Selection* (New York: Penguin Books, 2001), p. 642.

2. Arthur Middleton Reeves, North Ludlow Beamish, and Rasmus B. Anderson, *The Norse Discovery of America,* http://www.sacred-texts.com/neu/nda/nda08.htm

3. Modern History Sourcebook, *The Discovery of North America by Leif Eriksson, c. 1000, from* The Saga of Erik the Red, *1387,* http://www.fordham.edu/halsall/mod/1000Vinland.html

4. Ibid.

5. Ibid.

6. Thorsson, p. 643.

7. Reeves et al.

8. Ibid.

9. Ibid.

Chapter 5. Gudrid and Freydis

1. Örnólfur Thorsson, ed., *The Sagas of Icelanders: A Selection* (New York: Penguin Books, 2001), p. 647.

2. Modern History Sourcebook, *The Discovery of North America by Leif Eriksson, c. 1000, from* The Saga of Erik the Red, *1387,* http://www.fordham.edu/halsall/mod/1000Vinland.html

3. Ibid.

4. Ibid.

5. Thorsson, p. 650.

6. Ibid.

7. Ibid.

980	Leif Eriksson is born near present-day Budardalur, a small village at the head of Hvammsfjordur Bay in northwest Iceland, the second son of Erik the Red (Erik Thorvaldsson) and Thjodhild Jorundardottir.
981	Erik the Red is sentenced to outlawry for several killings (considered manslaughters) and banished from Iceland for three years.
982–984	Leif sails presumably from Iceland to Greenland with his family and spends three years there during his father's exile and exploration of the island.
985–986	Leif returns to Iceland from Greenland when his father's exile ends; goes back to Greenland with his family and a large expedition of settlers; settles with family at Brattahlid.
986–998	He spends boyhood years in Greenland (undocumented).
999	Leif sails from Greenland to Norway to visit King Olaf I Tryggvason; his ship is blown off course along the way and he spends the summer in the Hebrides; sails on to Norway and spends the winter in the court of Olaf I; converted to Christianity by Olaf I, who asks him to spread Christianity in Greenland upon his return.
1000	Leif returns to Greenland from Norway; spreads the word of Christianity; converts his mother, Thjodhild; decides to seek out the unknown lands to the west, which were sighted and reported earlier by Icelandic merchant Bjarni Herjolfsson; sails west and south from Greenland; discovers and names Helluland (Flat Rock Land), Markland (Forest Land), and Vinland (Vine or Wine Land), probably present-day Baffin Island, Labrador, and Newfoundland, respectively.
1001	Leif spends the winter in Vinland; sails for home in the spring; rescues fifteen shipwrecked Norwegian sailors on return voyage to Greenland; several of those rescued die of disease as his guests that winter at Brattahlid; Erik the Red also dies; Leif takes his father's place as paramount chieftain of Greenland.
1003	Leif's brother Thorvald leads an expedition to Vinland and spends two years there; Thorvald dies of a wound incurred in a skirmish with hostile natives.
1010	Icelandic explorer Thorfinn Karlsefni attempts to found a colony in North America.
c.1020	Leif Eriksson dies at Brattahlid; Thorkell, his son, succeeds him.

930	The *Althing,* the lawmaking assembly of Iceland, is founded by Norse settlers in Thingvellir.
945	Romanus I, co-emperor of the Byzantine Empire, is overthrown; Constantine VII rules alone until his death in 959.
962	Otto I, king of Saxony, is crowned Holy Roman Emperor.
964	New Maya Empire begins; ends c.1191.
976	St. Mark's Basilica in Venice is burned during a popular revolt against the doge.
983	Chinese of the Song Dynasty complete a multivolume encyclopedia.
985	Icelander Bjarni Herjolfsson sails along coast of North America after being blown off course on a voyage from Iceland to Greenland.
995	Olaf I Tryggvason conquers Norway and proclaims it a Christian kingdom.
1000	Olaf I, king of Norway, dies; Danes rule Norway.
1009	Muslims sack the Holy Sepulcher in Jerusalem.
1012	Persecution of heretics begins in Germany.
1015	Arabs conquer Sardinia.
1021	Epidemics of St. Vitus's Dance (Sydenham's chorea), a neurological disorder characterized by irregular and involuntary movements of various muscle groups, torment Europe.
1035	Castile becomes a separate kingdom.
1045	"El Cid" (Rodrigo Díaz de Vivar), Castilian military hero, is born; dies 1099.
1048	Persian poet and astronomer Omar Khayyam is born; dies 1131.
1050	The city of Oslo is founded in Norway.
1052	Edward the Confessor begins construction of Westminster Abbey in London.
1054	Final schism between western and eastern Christian churches occurs; Roman Catholic Church and Eastern Orthodox Church separate.
1057	Macbeth, king of Scots, is murdered by Malcolm and succeeded by his stepson Lulach.
1066	William, duke of Normandy, defeats Saxon King Harold at the Battle of Hastings.
1067	Work begins on Bayeux tapestry, which depicts the Battle of Hastings.
1070	Construction of York Cathedral begins in England.

FURTHER READING

Books

Burgan, Michael. *Leif Eriksson.* Portsmouth, New Hampshire: Heinemann, 2002.

Glaser, Jason. *Leif Eriksson.* Mankato, Minnesota: Capstone Press, 2005.

Kimmel, Elizabeth Cody. *Before Columbus: The Leif Eriksson Expedition.* New York: Random House, 2004.

Klingel, Cynthia Fitterer, and Robert B. Noyed. *Leif Eriksson: Norwegian Explorer.* Mankato, Minnesota: Child's World, 2002.

Mattern, Joanne. *Leif Eriksson: Viking Explorer.* Berkeley Heights, New Jersey: Enslow Publishers, 2004.

Works Consulted

Arbman, Holger. *The Vikings.* Translated and edited with an introduction by Alan Binns. New York: Barnes & Noble, 1995.

Batey, Colleen, Helen Clarke, R. I. Page, and Neil S. Price. *Cultural Atlas of the Viking World.* Edited by James Graham-Campbell. New York: Facts on File, 1994.

Batey, Colleen E., Judith Jesch, and Christopher D. Morris, eds. *The Viking Age in Caithness, Orkney and the North Atlantic.* Edinburgh, Scotland: Edinburgh University Press, 1995.

Bedini, Silvio A., ed. *Christopher Columbus and the Age of Exploration: An Encyclopedia.* New York: Da Capo Press, 1998.

Bohlander, Richard E., ed. *World Explorers and Discoverers.* New York: Da Capo Press, 1998.

Daniels, Patricia S., and Stephen G. Hyslop. *National Geographic Almanac of World History.* Washington, DC: National Geographic Society, 2003.

Davidson, H. R. Ellis. *Viking & Norse Mythology.* New York: Barnes & Noble, 1996.

Edmonds, Jane, ed. *Oxford Atlas of Exploration.* New York: Oxford University Press, 1997.

Fitzhugh, William W., and Elisabeth I. Ward, eds. *Vikings: The North Atlantic Saga.* Washington, DC: Smithsonian Institution Press, 2000.

Griffith, Paddy. *The Viking Art of War.* London: Greenhill Books, 1995.

Haywood, John. *Encyclopaedia of the Viking Age.* New York: Thames & Hudson, 2000.

———. *The Penguin Historical Atlas of the Vikings.* New York: Penguin Books, 1995.

Heath, Ian. *The Vikings.* Illustrated by Angus McBride. London: Osprey Publishing, 1999.

Jones, Gwyn. *A History of the Vikings.* Rev. ed. New York: Oxford University Press, 1984.

Kemp, Peter, ed. *The Oxford Companion to Ships and the Sea.* New York: Oxford University Press, 1988.

Marsden, John. *The Fury of the Northmen: Saints, Shrines and Sea-raiders in the Viking Age.* New York: St. Martin's Press, 1995.

Novaresio, Paolo. *The Explorers: From the Ancient World to the Present.* New York: Stewart, Tabori & Chang, 1996.

Orchard, Andy. *Dictionary of Norse Myth and Legend.* London: Cassell, 1997.

Page, R. I. *Chronicles of the Vikings: Records, Memorials and Myths.* New York: Barnes & Noble, 1995.

Salentiny, Fernand. *Encyclopedia of World Explorers: From Armstrong to Shackleton.* Edited by Werner Waldmann. London: Dumont Monte, 2003.

Sawyer, P. H. *Kings and Vikings: Scandinavia and Europe, A.D. 700–1100.* New York: Barnes & Noble, 1994.

Sawyer, Peter, ed. *The Oxford Illustrated History of the Vikings.* New York: Oxford University Press, 1997.

Thorsson, Örnólfur, ed. *The Sagas of Icelanders: A Selection.* New York: Penguin Books, 2001.

Toyne, S. M. *The Scandinavians in History.* New York: Barnes & Noble, 1996.

Wilson, David M. *The Vikings and Their Origins: Scandinavia in the First Millennium.* New York: Thames & Hudson, 1991.

On the Internet

Modern History Sourcebook: *The Discovery of North America by Leif Eriksson, c. 1000, from* The Saga of Erik the Red, *1387* http://www.fordham.edu/halsall/mod/1000Vinland.html

PBS: *The Viking Deception* http://www.pbs.org/wgbh/nova/vinland

Reeves, Arthur Middleton, North Ludlow Beamish, and Rasmus B. Anderson. *The Norse Discovery of America,* "A Brief History of Erik the Red" http://www.sacred-texts.com/neu/nda/nda08.htm

Sephton, John, translator. *The Project Gutenberg eBook of* Eirik the Red's Saga, *by Anonymous* http://www.gutenberg.org/files/17946/17946-h/17946-h.htm

GLOSSARY

Age of Discovery—A period of transoceanic exploration that began in the early 1400s and extended into the early 1600s; sometimes referred to as the Age of Exploration.

Brattahlid (BRAAT-tah-lid)—Farmstead of Erik the Red and his family overlooking Eiriksfjord (ehr-iks-FEE-ord) (Erik's inlet) in Greenland.

knörr (NOHR)—A Viking merchant ship modeled on the traditional longship, with one mast and a single square sail set on a yard.

Helluland—Flat Rock Land; site of Leif Eriksson's first landing in North America; now believed to be Baffin Island.

Markland—Forest Land; site of Leif Eriksson's second landing in North America; usually identified as present-day Labrador.

pagan (PAY-gun)—Heathen; one who believes in many gods or has little or no religion.

skraeling (SKREL-ing)—Unflattering Norse term for Amerindians or Inuits.

Viking Age—The period of Viking raids and expansion, beginning c.800 and ending c.1100.

Vikings—Scandinavian sea rovers who raided and colonized areas of Europe and the North Atlantic during the ninth through the eleventh centuries; also known as Norsemen or Northmen.

Vinland—Vine Land, Wine Land, or Meadow Land; unidentified site of Leif Eriksson's third landing in North America; now generally believed to be either Newfoundland or Massachusetts.

INDEX